sport an alternative perspective

mad
moose
press

Managing Editors: Simon Melhuish and Emma Craven
Series Editor: Lee Linford
Contributors: Simon Melhuish, Emma Craven, Lee Linford, Nikole G. Bamford

Design: Alan Shiner
Illustrations: Justine Waldie
Photography: Getty Images (excl. p39)

Designed and compiled by
Mad Moose Press
for
Lagoon Books
PO Box 311, KT2 5QW, UK
PO Box 990676, Boston, MA 02199, USA

ISBN: 1-904139-17-5

www.madmoosepress.com
www.lagoongames.com

Printed in China.

It's blood, sweat, sometimes tears.
Bob Hayes

The man who can drive himself farther once the effort gets painful is the man who will win.
Roger Bannister

It's just a job. Grass grows, birds fly, waves pound the sand. I just beat people up.
Muhammad Ali

Looking for action? Join the club.

When it comes to sport, everyone has an
opinion. Here's a book with some views all of its
own, tackling sport from another direction;
bending the rules just a little further.

Prepare yourself for an unconventional visual
journey into the competitive world of
professional sport, punctuated with a few
words of wisdom and some rather more
conventional explanations.

home run ▸ *noun* (Baseball) a strike of the ball that enables the player to run the full circuit of bases, scoring a run.

Mexican wave ▶ *noun* a wave or ripple effect produced by a crowd of people in a stadium or arena, created when a large section successively stand up with their arms raised, before lowering them and sitting down.

supporters

Every crowd has a silver lining.

P. T. Barnum

substitute ▸ *noun* something or someone used as a replacement for a similar item or person; a teacher who replaces another teacher in their absence; (sports) a player brought on during the course of a game to replace another player; *verb* to replace an item or person for an alternative; act as a replacement; take on the role of replacing another player during a game.

hat-trick ▸ *noun* achievement of three consecutive successes, especially in sport; (soccer) the scoring of three goals by an individual player in one match; (cricket) the taking of three wickets with consecutive balls by a single bowler.

train

If you train hard, you'll not only be hard, you'll be hard to beat.

Herschel Walker

warm up

warm up

big match ▶ *noun* a competitive event of significance, usually between two teams of similar skill or repute or between teams that are historically competitive.

Ask not what your teammates can do for you. Ask what you can do for your teammates.

Magic Johnson

team selection

foul ▸ *adjective* extremely unpleasant odor or taste; unpleasant or objectionable: *a foul mood*; offensive language; harsh weather conditions (esp. wet or stormy); immoral or evil; acting against the rules of a sport; polluted or tainted: *the water had been fouled with chemical waste*; ***noun*** an unfair or invalid act of play in contravention to the rules of a sport, often causing injury to or interfering with another player; a collision or entanglement usually in running, riding or rowing; ***verb*** to taint or make dirty; to entangle or collide; to commit an unfair act of play in a sport.

track

track

line-up ▸ *noun* queue of people waiting in a line; objects arranged in a line; selected group of people, often a sports team, assembled for a specific purpose (such as taking part in a competitive event); a group of people preparing to compete (in a race); *verb* organize or arrange something for an event or occasion.

strike zone ▸ *noun* (Baseball) term for an imaginary area above the homeplate that extends from a player's chest to their knees when in the batting position, awaiting delivery of the ball.

strike zone

racket

tackle ▶ *noun* equipment or accessories required for a particular sport, task or game, especially fishing; a rope and pulley mechanism devised to lift heavy weights, sails or other items; (soccer & hockey) the act of intercepting a ball in an opponent's possession; (American football & rugby) the act of grappling an opposing player to prevent their progress with the ball; (American football) a player positioned next to the end of the forward line; *verb* (soccer & hockey) attempt to intercept and prevent an opponent from advancing with the ball by playing it whilst in their possession; (American football & rugby) grab hold of and bring an opposing player to the ground to prevent progress with the ball; attempt to resolve or handle a tricky problem, situation or question.

captain ▶ *noun* a middle ranking military officer above lieutenant (US); a high ranking naval officer above commander; a person responsible for commanding a ship or civilian aircraft; a police officer responsible for a precinct, reporting to a chief officer; a senior fire department officer; a person leading a team, particularly a sports team; someone of power and influence within a specific field: *a captain of industry*. *verb* the act of being in charge of or responsible for the overall organization and play of a sports team (esp. during competition); to be in control or in charge of an aircraft or ship.

captain

Coaches have to watch for what they don't want to see and listen to what they don't want to hear.

John Madden

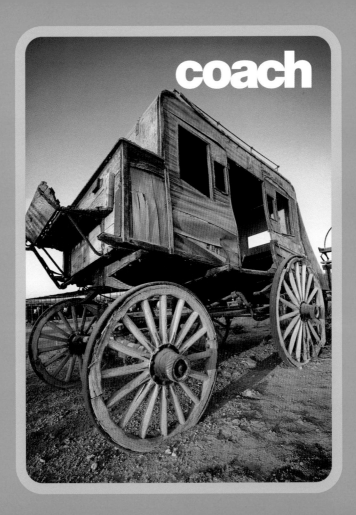

touchdown

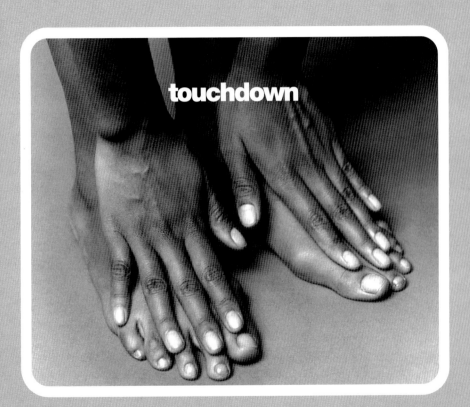

offside ▸ *adjective & adverb* (sporting term, esp. in hockey, rugby or soccer) referring to a player illegally positioned on the field, ahead of the ball (or puck), whereby play may be affected should the ball be passed.

offside

penalty ▶ *noun* a punishment or fine imposed for breaking an agreement, contract, ruling or law; (in sports, esp. ice hockey & soccer) a handicap or disadvantage imposed on a team or player as a result of breaking or infringing the rules of the game; a shot given to a team as compensation for an opponent's infringement of the game's rules.

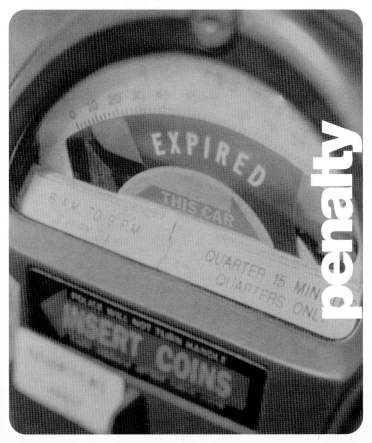

EXPIRED

THIS CAR

8 AM TO 9 PM

QUARTER 15 MIN
QUARTERS ONLY

INSERT COINS

penalty

fans ▶ *noun* someone with considerable enthusiasm or interest in a specific sport, sports team, personality or art form: *he was a dedicated baseball fan.*

pitcher

pitcher

dribble ▸ *verb* slow movement of a liquid in small quantities; allow saliva to escape from the mouth; (basketball, hockey & soccer) progress past opponents with the ball by either continuous bouncing against the ground (basketball), successive light touches with the stick (hockey) or small, controlled kicks (soccer); *noun* a trickle of liquid; saliva allowed to run from the mouth; an act of forwards movement with a ball (basketball, hockey & soccer); nonsensical statement(s) or view(s).

sending-off ▶ *noun* (sporting term) an act by which a player is dismissed from a game for committing a foul (or fouls)

sending-off

tight **end** ▸ *noun* (American football) an offensive end who lines up close to a tackle.

tight end

shoot

You miss 100% of the shots you never take.

Wayne Gretzky

great catch

great catch

relay ▶ *noun* a team or group (usually people or animals) employed to carry out an activity for a period of time before being replaced by a relief team; a team race, usually running or swimming, in which each team member successively completes part of the overall race: *the USA won the gold for the Olympic 400m relay*; an electrical component used to control electrical circuits; a broadcasting device used to transmit messages; *verb* to pass on received information; to re-broadcast signals received from another transmitter.

striker ▶ *noun* (sports) a player who's purpose in a game is to strike the ball; (soccer) an attacking or forward player.

sin bin ▶ *noun* (sporting term) an area off the field of play, especially in ice hockey, where a player may be sent for a specified period of time upon committing an offense against the rules of the game.

sin bin

score

final ▶ *adjective* the last in a series; allowing no further doubt or discussion; *noun* the last and deciding game, match or race at the end of a sports tournament or competition; an end of year test or examination taken at school; (UK) examination taken upon completion of a degree course..

talent scout ▶ *noun* any individual employed to search for talented or gifted people, especially those with sporting talent.

talent scout

personal best

If you set a goal for yourself and are able to achieve it, you have won your own race. Your goal can be to come first, to improve your performance, or just finish the race - it's up to you.

Dave Scott

personal best

finishing line

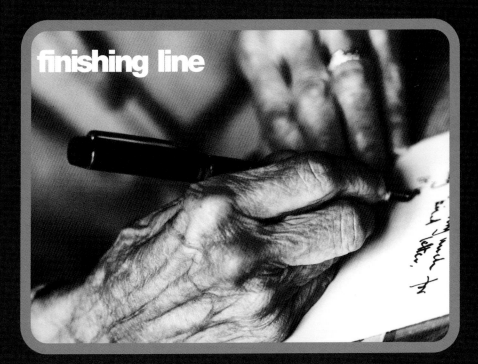

finishing line

tiebreak ▶ _noun_ (tennis) an extra game played to decide the final outcome of a set when competitors are tied at six games all.

bronze ▶ *noun* metal alloy made from copper and tin, bright brown in color; a color resembling the metal in appearance; a statue or sculpture made from the alloy; a small metal disk made of bronze, presented to the third placed competitor or team in a competition (bronze medal); *verb* the act of tanning a part of the body in the sun; coat or cover something to make it bronze in appearance.

bronze

gold ▸ *noun* a soft precious metal, yellow and shiny in appearance, used extensively in jewelry and for decoration *(atomic symbol: Au)*; an alloy containing gold; a color resembling the metal in color or appearance; a metal disk made of gold, awarded as a prize to the winning competitor or team in an event or competition (gold medal).

cheerleader

When the going gets tough, the tough get going.

close match

When the going gets tough,
the tough get going.

Proverb

coverage

coverage

world record

Adversity causes some men to break; others to break records.

William A. Ward

world record

final whistle ▶ *noun* (sporting term) a whistle blown to signify the end of a competitive game or match, esp. in hockey, rugby or soccer.

final whistle

cheers

Men seek less to be instructed than applauded.

Proverb

final whistle

cheers

Men seek less to be
instructed than applauded.

Proverb

Look out for the other titles in the Thought Provokers range:

Thought Provokers - LOVE
Thought Provokers - LIFE